Canadian Wilderness

THE POWER, SCENERY & SPIRIT OF THE NORTH

CANWEST BOOKS

Published by CanWest Books Inc.
A subsidiary of CanWest MediaWorks Publications Inc.
1450 Don Mills Road
Toronto, ON
Canada, M3B 2X7

Library and Archives Canada Cataloguing in Publication

Thomson, Tom, 1957-
Canadian wilderness : the power, scenery, and spirit
of the North / author/photographer: Tom Thomson ;
editor: Kerry MacGregor ; designer: Rob Dokuchie.

ISBN 0-9736719-9-8

1. Wilderness areas--Ontario, Northern--Pictorial works. 2. Ontario,
Northern--Pictorial works. I. MacGregor, Kerry, 1976- II. Title.

FC3094.4.T45 2005   917.13'1'00222   C2005-903874-8

Book Design: Rob Dokuchie, Overdrive Design Labs Inc.
Prepress: Emerson Group
Photography: Tom Thomson

Printed and Bound in Canada by Tri-Graphic

First Edition

10 9 8 7 6 5 4 3 2 1

Canadian Wilderness

THE POWER, SCENERY & SPIRIT OF THE NORTH

Canadian Wilderness

THE POWER, SCENERY & SPIRIT OF THE NORTH

The national identity of Canadians has largely been shaped by the space that surrounds us — by our diverse landscapes, our picturesque waterways and our abundant wilderness.

As a child growing up in the bush, I was always on the lake, always outdoors. My father worked as a fishing guide and I had my own boat at the age of 15. I was constantly in awe of the nature that was around me.

As an adult, when I picked up a camera years later, I was lucky enough to see that wilderness all new again. And I am still in awe.

My early introduction to the wilderness taught me a great deal. It taught me tolerance and understanding; I learned how to respect nature and how not to use it up. Many people go through life without a rear-view mirror, but Canada's natural heritage teaches us to look all around us.

Photographing nature, I have learned, is somewhat like fishing. The old saying that a bad day of fishing is better than a good day at work applies to what I do, as it did my father's passion. I am willing to wait hours for a photo. And if I don't get anything, at least I was out in the woods all day. Any day spent in the woods is a good one.

In many ways, the wilderness *is* the Canadian identity. The distance around our communities, I believe, is what provides us with our gentle nature. We aren't so crowded together; we have room to breathe.

It is this breathing room that, every year, attracts visitors to this country from around the world. They come to view our scenery, swim in our waters and gaze at our wildlife. I consider myself lucky to be able to go out my back door and experience that nature each day. That's why I live where I live. And the career I have chosen, I am grateful to say, makes the most of that opportunity.

To me, there is no point in taking a photograph that goes unseen. I love to share the images I have collected - whether I'm zooming in on that little detail or watching how the light changes.

Canadian Wilderness is a collection of some of my favourite photographs from across the country. I hope these images will inspire people to travel to these places. I hope they will evoke some emotion and give some idea of the beauty this country holds. But in no way is this book to be seen as a definitive collection of what Canada has to offer - it is merely a sampling.

There's a lot of wilderness in Canada, and I hope to travel to every part of it I can. I haven't seen enough of it yet.

– Tom Thomson

Early-morning mist on a lake near
Minaki, Ontario

The Power, Scenery & Spirit of the North

Pelicans preening on a summer
evening, Winnipeg River, Ontario

Caribou near the Kazan River,
Nunavut

Silver Lake, Ontario

Stream near Banff, Alberta

Reeds, northwestern
Ontario

Sunset, Lake of the Woods,
Ontario

Aerial view of a creek near
Red Lake, Ontario

White-tailed deer (does) on
farmland near Laclu, Ontario

Ice-fishing shack at nearly
40-below, Lake of the Woods,
Ontario

Ice forming on Lake of the Woods,
Ontario

Frosty maple seeds near Kenora,
Ontario

New ice that formed overnight
on Lake of the Woods,
Ontario

Stand of pine trees in
Redditt, Ontario

Kakabeca Falls,
Ontario

Mist at the mouth of the Winnipeg
River at 40-below, Kenora, Ontario

Silver Lake shoreline,
Ontario

Marsh, northwestern
Ontario

Sunset near Winnipeg, Manitoba

Stream near Kananaskis,
Alberta

Canada goose, Winnipeg River,
Ontario

Milkweed, Nunavut

Pine and spruce trees in a marsh
near Vermillion Bay, Ontario

Badlands, Alberta

Sunrise over a peninsula, Lake of the Woods, Ontario

Inukshuk, Rankin Inlet, Nunavut

Prairie near Drumheller,
Alberta

Bull moose swimming, Umperville
Lake, Ontario

Bull moose, Alberta

The Rocky Mountains near
Kananaskis, Alberta

Rapids on a rainy day in
northwestern Ontario

Aerial view of Hudson Bay near
Rankin Inlet, Nunavut

Waterfall, Alberta

Sow bear in a tree,
Kenora, Ontario

Sunset over Kazan River,
Nunavut

Poplar trees near Prawda,
Manitoba

Sunrise over a dock in
northwestern Ontario

Misty morning, Laclu, Ontario

Spring snowstorm, Kenora,
Ontario

Tree surrounded by a blanket of
snow on Lake of the Woods,
Ontario

Rushing River, Rushing River
Provincial Park, Ontario

Snowdrift at Rushing River,
Rushing River Provincial Park,
Ontario

Sunrise through steam from the open water, Coney Island, Kenora, Ontario

Foliage growing out of the rocky
shoreline, Alberta

Caribou antlers, evening, Yathkyed
Lake, Nunavut

Badlands, Alberta

Prairie dog, Manitoba

Great Grey Owl near Thunder Bay,
Ontario

Bald eagle flying away from a deer carcass, northwestern Ontario

Vegetation under the water at the mouth of a river, northwestern Ontario

Sunset, northwestern
Ontario

Northern lights near Falcon Lake,
Manitoba

Loon in morning mist, surrounded
by trees that died during flooding
for a power dam, Umperville Lake,
Ontario

Lily pads in early morning on a
small, unnamed lake near Sioux
Narrows, Ontario

Aerial view of rapids near Berens
River, Ontario

Birch tree near Sioux Lookout,
Ontario

Sunset over Winnipeg River,
Ontario

Dusk on Lake of the Woods,
Ontario

Lake of the Woods begins to
freeze, Ontario

Sunset on Winnipeg River,
Ontario

Canola field northeast of Selkirk,
Manitoba

Sunset through the grass, Nunavut

Grass in Minaki, Ontario

Bulrushes, Dowswell Lake, Ontario

Painted turtles, Turtle Bay, Lake of
the Woods, Ontario

Canoe in bulrushes, northwestern
Ontario

Bulrushes in the evening, Laclu, Ontario

Ice forming in reeds, Lake of the Woods, Ontario

The Power, Scenery & Spirit of the North

White-tailed deer (buck) near
Kenora, Ontario, evening

White-tailed deer near Winnipeg
River, Ontario

The Power, Scenery & Spirit of the North

Lily pads near Kenora, Ontario

Island in the evening on Lake of
the Woods, Ontario

The Power, Scenery & Spirit of the North

Rushing River, Rushing River
Provincial Park, Ontario

Opposite: Re-growth after a forest
fire near Minaki, Ontario

The Power, Scenery & Spirit of the North

Seagull at sunrise, Lake of the
Woods, Ontario

Canada geese in flight, Winnipeg
River, Ontario

Great blue heron, northwestern
Ontario

An evening on the Winnipeg River,
Ontario

Aerial view near Red Lake, Ontario

Sunset through pine trees,
northwestern Ontario

Sunset through spruce trees,
northwestern Ontario

The Power, Scenery & Spirit of the North

Sunset, northwestern Ontario

Grass in Manitoba

The Power, Scenery & Spirit of the North

The Rocky Mountains, Alberta

Rapids on the Kazan River,
Nunavut

The Power, Scenery & Spirit of the North

Canadian Wilderness

Geese in mist, northwestern
Ontario

Great blue heron wading,
Winnipeg River, Ontario

Caribou, Kazan River,
Nunavut

Lake in northwestern Ontario

Cedar trees, Lake of the Woods,
Ontario

Bird near the Berens River, south of Hudson Bay, Ontario

Bald eagle fishing, Lake of the
Woods, Ontario

Sunrise over the Kazan River,
Nunavut

Poplar trees, northwestern Ontario

Creek, northwestern
Ontario

Prairie dog, Nunavut

Cedar trees near Lac La Croix, on
the western edge of Quetico
Provincial Park, Ontario

Caribou, Nunavut

Northern lights over
Berens River, Ontario

Winnipeg River, Ontario

Mist over Lake of the Woods,
Ontario

Marsh in northern Ontario

The Power, Scenery & Spirit of the North

Loon, Winnipeg River, Ontario

Reeds in the morning on Lake of
the Woods, Ontario

Lac Seul, Ontario

Wildflowers, Lake of the Woods,
Ontario

Lake of the Woods,
Ontario